From the desktop of Jeffrey Simmons

A vacation in Paris inspired Miroslav Sasek to create children's travel guides to the big cities of the world. He brought me *This is Paris* in 1958 when I was publishing in London, and we soon followed up with *This is London*. Both books were enormously successful, and his simple vision grew to include more than a dozen books. Their amusing verse, coupled with bright and charming illustrations, made for a series unlike any other, and garnered Sasek (as we always called him) the international and popular acclaim he deserved.

I was thrilled to learn that *This is Greece* will once again find its rightful place on bookshelves. Sasek is no longer with us (and I have lost all contact with his family), but I am sure he would be delighted to know that a whole new generation of wide-eyed readers is being introduced to his whimsical, imaginative, and enchanting world.

_____

Your name here

Published by arrangement with Simon & Schuster Books for Young Readers,
Simon & Schuster Children's Publishing Division

This edition first published in the United States of America in 2009 by
UNIVERSE PUBLISHING
A Division of Rizzoli International Publications, Inc.
300 Park Avenue South
New York, NY 10010
www.rizzoliusa.com

*See updated Greece facts at end of book

2009 2010 2011 2012 2013 / 10 9 8 7 6 5 4 3 2 1

Printed in China

ISBN–13: 978-0-7893-1855-8

Library of Congress Control Number: 2008933180

Cover design: Sara Stemen

M·SASEK

THIS IS
GREECE

UNIVERSE

Greece, rich in history, in light, in marble; the birthplace of western civilization. What Odysseus said of Ithaca can be said of all Greece: "a small place, but a good place for breeding men." It is a land of mountains (the highest, Olympus, 9,577 feet), of coastline, and of islands which are themselves mountains rooted in the sea. This topography greatly influenced Greek history: the mountain barriers tended to separate the Greek city-states from each other, to protect them from the northern barbarians, and to send the Hellenes southeastward and seaward for new places to trade and to live. Today the area of Greece is 50,944 square miles, and the population 11.2 million, of whom 3.37 million people live in the capital, Athens.

Most of what Greece has given to the world ancient Athens gave to Greece. The greatest glory of the city-state of Athens lasted only about a century (from c. 480 to c. 380 B.C.),* and her population totaled about 350,000 all of Attica (about the area of Gloucestershire or Rhode Island). Yet Athens gave to the theater Aeschylus, Sophocles, Euripides, and Aristophanes, to oratory Demosthenes, to statecraft and strategy Solon, Themistocles, Aristides, Pericles, to history-writing Thucydides, to sculpture Phidias and Praxiteles, to philosophy Socrates and Plato.

Athens is named after the most ancient protectress of the city, the goddess Athena, whose vast statue, covered in ivory and gold, stood inside her temple, the Parthenon, on the Acropolis.

Athena was the daughter of Zeus. She emerged fully grown from his brow one fine Olympian day.

"You should fix your eyes on the greatness of Athens and should fall in love with her." Pericles (c. 495–429 B.C.), who thus exhorted his fellow citizens, inspired and largely carried out the magnificent rebuilding of the Acropolis which had been destroyed by the Persians in 480 B.C. This is how it looked to the Athenians, who thereafter took his advice.

"Mighty indeed are the marks and monuments which we have left. Future ages will wonder at us." —Pericles.

Pericles

The mightiest monument, the Parthenon, the supreme example of Doric style, the marvel of classical architecture. It remained almost intact until 1687 when a Venetian cannon shot blew up Turkish munitions stored inside. The Venetian gun stood at the same place from which we are looking, the summit of the Philopappos, in ancient times the Hill of the Muses.

View of the Acropolis from the Areopagus. "Acro polis"
simply means "high town"— a fortress, a place of wor-
ship. Many Greek cities have one.

The Propylaea, the monumental gateway to the Acropolis.
On the precipitous platform at the right stands the Temple
of Nike (Victory), commemorating the defeat of the Persians
by the Greeks.

The Areopagus, or Hill of Ares (Mars), gave its name to a
council of nobles which met there.

There too, in 54 A.D., St. Paul preached to the Athenians.

The Erechtheion, raised near the
spot where, according to legend,
the goddess Athena fought with the
sea god Poseidon for possession
of the city.

The Parthenon at the summit of the Acropolis,
grandiose in a sea of shattered marble.

The Propylaea.

A tourist photographing a photogra-
pher photographing tourists against
the Parthenon.

On the northern slope of the Acropolis is the "Plaka," the
old popular quarter of Athens. Its many taverns often put
their tables and chairs in rather improbable places.

On the southern slope of the Acropolis is the Theatre of Dionysus (originally built of wood), where the plays of Aeschylus, Sophocles, Euripides, and Aristophanes were first performed.

Statuette of a tragic hero.

Greek theater was highly stylized. Actors wore padded costumes, masks, and boots with heavy wooden blocks for soles (cothurnus). The height of the cothurnus varied with the importance of the character.

The Agora (marketplace) was the center of the public life of ancient Greek cities. The Athenian Agora lies under the north side of the Acropolis.

A view of the Agora from the Theseion. The Stoa in the background, reconstructed by American archaeologists, houses an interesting collection of articles from the daily life of the ancient Greeks. The original Stoa of Attalus (2nd Century B.C.) had its roofed colonnade backed by shops and offices.

One of the exhibits — a pottie 25 centuries old.

The Temple of Hephaestus (Vulcan), mistakenly called the Theseion after the Athenian hero Theseus whose bones are supposedly buried somewhere nearby. It is the best preserved temple in Greece.

The Athenians were great talkers. They talked all sorts of business and settled in the Agora; state business was discussed and settled in the Assembly. The Assembly met monthly at the Pnyx. Every male citizen was a member and had the right to speak. Here the Orator-statesmen of Athens—Themistocles, Aristides, Pericles, Demosthenes—won their leadership of the city, by persuasion.

The remains of the largest temple in Greece, the Temple of Olympian Zeus.

Begun by the enlightened Athenian "tyrant" Pisistratus in the 6th Century B.C.; finished by the Roman Emperor Hadrian in 130 A.D.

One of the pillars of the temple, conveniently broken down by nature into its component parts for students of architecture.

The potters' district, the Kerameikos, gave its name to a burying place used from the early Bronze Age. It was the chief cemetery of Athens from late Mycenaean times until the 4th Century B.C. The graves are outside the Sacred Gate and the Dipylon gate of old Athens. The Sacred Way, lined with tombs and monuments, led towards the ritual city of Eleusis. In workshops near the Dipylon Gate, famous Greek vases were made from the 9th Century B.C. onwards.*

This is the typical "Dipylon" style of 9th Century decoration, a geometrical pattern with simplified human figures.

The Syntagma Square, the heart of modern Athens. Hotels, cafés, air terminals. In the background, the Parliament. From its balcony the Greek constitution was proclaimed in 1843.

In modern Greece as in ancient, much of life is lived in the open air.

lots of luck at every corner—
lottery tickets on sticks.

self-propelled sponges

At the street side the friendly, hard-working
Greeks will—feed you

photograph you

clean or repair for you

shield your eyes

provision you

button you.

29

Though modern Greek differs widely from old, the alphabet is mostly unchanged. Some other things also have not changed. The ancient "barbaros" (barbarian, foreigner) meant a person who, instead of speaking Greek, made noises like "bar-bar."

Many present-day tourists make the same noises.

The official Church is the Greek Orthodox.

Next to the modern Cathedral and well below street level stands the "Small Metropolis," the old Byzantine Cathedral from the 12th Century.

Icons are everywhere, even in buses and trucks.

Greece is a constitutional monarchy. On duty outside the Royal Palace are picturesque Evzones, the Royal Guards.

Other varieties of picturesque national costumes—and two variants of the national flag:

This one is flown in seaports and foreign countries. Its nine stripes are said to symbolize the nine syllables of the Greek motto: "Liberty or Death."

This simple one is flown in Greece.

Where the ancient stadium stood, a modern one was built for the revival of the Olympic Games which took place there in 1896. It was finished in 1906.

Piraeus has been the port of Athens since antiquity. It is the largest port in Greece. It was linked with the city by the "Long Walls" in the 5th Century B.C. Today the walls are in ruins, but Piraeus still forms one city with Athens.

Invaders of mountain-locked Greece have generally come by sea.

The tomb of the 192 Athenian heroes who fell at Marathon.

In 490 B.C. at Marathon, a small Athenian army under Miltiades heavily defeated an invading Persian force. The enemy ships then set course for Athens itself, around Cape Sunion. But the Greek victors ran from the battlefield across country to the port, got there first, and prevented another landing.

The helmet of Miltiades (in the museum at Olympia).*

The tomb of the 300 Spartans at Thermopylae, with the statue of their leader, Leonidas.

In 480 B.C. the Persians—in millions—attacked again. At the Pass of Thermopylae a handful of Spartans bravely fought the invaders, but were finally betrayed and killed.

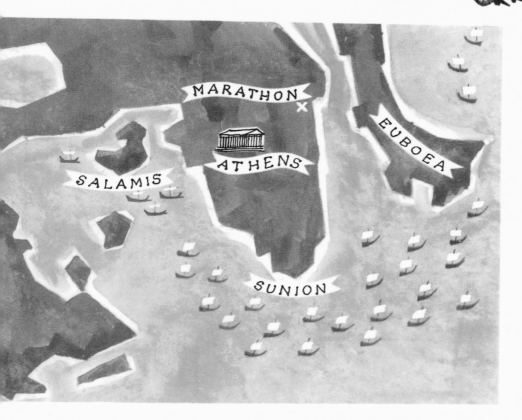

Then, however, the vast Persian armada was destroyed at the glorious battle of Salamis, near Piraeus, by a much smaller—mainly Athenian—fleet.

The hero of the battle was the warrior—statesman Themistocles. This victory determined the whole course of our history and culture.*

Daphni.

Not far from here Xerxes, the Persian King, watched from a golden throne the destruction of his fleet at Salamis. Here originally was a sanctuary of Apollo. The monastery, founded in the 6th Century A.D., owes its name to the laurels—"dafnai"—sacred to Apollo, which grew all around.

The 11th Century Byzantine church contains exquisite mosaics.

The Corinth Canal was dug in 1893 at the narrowest point of the Isthmus between the mainland and the Peloponnesus. Already in antiquity there had been many plans thus to shorten the sea route—Nero actually inaugurated the work with a golden shovel in 67 A.D.—but none of the projects was carried through. The ancient Hellenes used to drag their ships overland at this place from one sea to the other. Crossing the canal we enter the Peloponnesus, the "Isle of Pelop."

The Peloponnesus, virtually an island, had surprisingly little communication with the sea; its few good harbors had almost no hinterland.

Corinth, at the Peloponnesian end of the Isthmus, astride both land and sea routes, grew important and wealthy. The pleasure city of ancient Greece; in Roman times visited by apostles, emperors, philosophers, and earthquakes; destroyed by the last in 521 A.D. Its painted vases and its ornate style of architecture are famous.

The Temple of Apollo
(6th Century B.C.)

41

The Lion Gate, built at the peak of the glory of Mycenae, as were the citadel and the palace beyond.

Mycenae, one of the most ancient sites of the Peloponnesus, inhabited already in 3000 B.C. Its greatest period came in the Late Bronze Age (1400–1150 B.C.). After the Trojan War (1194–1184 B.C.) it declined. The Greek army in that war was commanded by Agamemnon, the King of Mycenae, the son of Atreus, and grandson of Pelops, who gave his name to the peninsula. The heroic deeds of the war are described by Homer in the *Iliad*.

The Treasury of Atreus, also called the Tomb of Agamemnon, an astonishing masterpiece of this period.

"I have seen the face of Agamemnon," exulted the archaeologist Schliemann when he unearthed this golden death-mask in a Mycenaean tomb. But it turned out to come from even earlier times. The mask and many other Mycenaean treasures are now in the Archaeological Museum in Athens.

Epidaurus, the most renowned spa of ancient Greece, centered around the sanctuary of Asclepius, hero and god of healing. It is chiefly known for its magnificent theater (4th Century B.C.), which is still used today for festival performances of ancient Greek drama.

Nauplia, important in antiquity, was briefly the capital of Greece in modern times (1829–1934).

The island off its shore was reserved for retired executioners. Today their forbidding home has been turned into a luxurious hotel.

Olympia, originally sacred to the most ancient goddess Gaea (the Earth), in classical times the main sanctuary of Zeus in Greece, lies in the loveliest part of the Peloponnesus, the Elis. Here the pan-Hellenic Olympic Games were held every four years from 776 B.C. to c. 393 A.D. To win the first prize—a crown of wild olive leaves—was the most urgent ambition of every young Hellene. Victory in the games brought the greatest public honor; statues of victorious athletes were placed in the sacred precinct, the Olympic Altis. The sacred truce that was always declared during the Games meant that at least for a while all Hellenes were united.

ΣΤΟΑ
ΗΧΟΥΣ

The athletes' entrance to the Stadium.

The hill of Kronos, son of Heaven and Earth, and father of Zeus.

The Olympic Stadium with the original starting line.

The museum of Olympia houses some of the most celebrated sculptures of ancient Greece, above all the Hermes of Praxiteles.

Delphi, a sacred spot since remote antiquity, in classical times the location of the supreme Delphic oracle of the Hellenes, is situated on the slopes of Mount Parnassus, high above the Gulf of Corinth, on the Greek mainland, amidst astounding scenery.

From a terrace above the theater, a view towards the Temple of Apollo. The Holy of Holies was located beneath the temple. Here the famous Pythian priestess uttered her prophecies under the guidance of Apollo. The oracle had tremendous influence on the whole Greek world.

The Sacred Way, lined by the treasuries of Greek city-states, winds up to the temple from the road below.

The reconstructed Athenian Treasury, originally consecrated in 300 B.C. and endowed with the spoils from Marathon. Pythia's rock-seat is close by.

The "omphalos" (navel stone) originally placed at the "center of the earth," the Holy of Holies, is now to be found in the museum at Delphi.

The stadium, together with the theater and the hippodrome, was built for the Pythian Games, founded in 582 B.C. at Delphi. The prize was a laurel wreath.

A view of the modern town of Delphi with 4,000,000 olive trees in the valley below.

The town of Kalabaka.

The "Meteora" (the monasteries in the air) in Thessaly, one of the curiosities of Greece. The monasteries, clinging to the narrow summits of precipitous rocks, were founded in the war-torn 14th Century. Today most of them are uninhabited.

The Meteora can now be reached by road from Kalabaka, by footpaths and rocky stairs.

Previously the monks had to use this method of transport.

The Greek islands are many, 1,425 in all. Only 166 of them are inhabited.*

Picturesque Hydra, the 18th Century refuge of Albanian pirates. Today frequented mainly by tourists and artists, and by the Athenian owners of some of the island's fine old houses.

Mykonos, in the midst of the Cyclades, known for its pretty windmills—

its snow-white streets—

and its patron pelican Petra.

Delos was already inhabited in prehistoric times. It was sacred to Apollo who, according to legend, was born under this palm which still today is the only tree on the arid isle.

From 478 to 454 B.C. the Treasury of the Delian League was kept at Delos. The league was organized, under the leadership of Athens, as a permanent defensive and offensive alliance against Persia. In 426 B.C. Athens purified the island, a ceremony which included the banning of births or deaths on its sacred soil. Women in labor or people about to die were hastily taken to a neighboring island. By the beginning of our era the island was abandoned.*

The row of marble lions (7th Century B.C.), overlooking the Sacred Lake.

The sanctuary of Isis on the western slope of Mt. Cynthos.

The famous bronze statue (c. 470 B.C.) of Poseidon, the god of the sea, was found—appropriately—in the sea.* It is now at the Archaeological Museum in Athens.

Sunion (Sunium), a promontory at the southern tip of Attica, crowned by a temple of Poseidon (5th Century B.C.). The time to visit this temple is at sunset.

In the awe-inspiring places where so much of what we all now possess was thought or done for the first time, the ancient gods still do appear to those who have the eyes to see.

For Greece is the land of gods and heroes as well as of philosophers and statesmen, a land of intellectual light as well as of mysterious dusk.

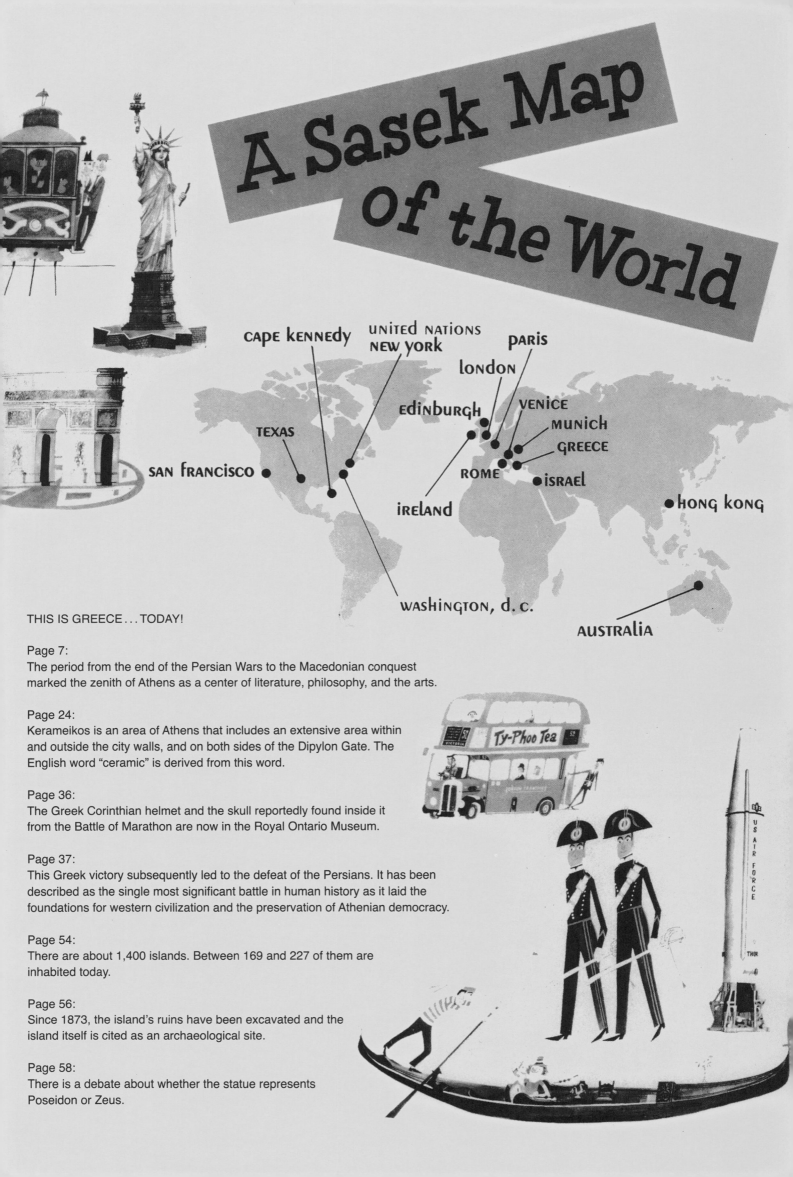

A Sasek Map of the World

CAPE KENNEDY
UNITED NATIONS NEW YORK
PARIS
LONDON
EDINBURGH
VENICE
MUNICH
TEXAS
GREECE
SAN FRANCISCO
ROME
ISRAEL
IRELAND
HONG KONG
WASHINGTON, D. C.
AUSTRALIA

THIS IS GREECE...TODAY!

Page 7:
The period from the end of the Persian Wars to the Macedonian conquest marked the zenith of Athens as a center of literature, philosophy, and the arts.

Page 24:
Kerameikos is an area of Athens that includes an extensive area within and outside the city walls, and on both sides of the Dipylon Gate. The English word "ceramic" is derived from this word.

Page 36:
The Greek Corinthian helmet and the skull reportedly found inside it from the Battle of Marathon are now in the Royal Ontario Museum.

Page 37:
This Greek victory subsequently led to the defeat of the Persians. It has been described as the single most significant battle in human history as it laid the foundations for western civilization and the preservation of Athenian democracy.

Page 54:
There are about 1,400 islands. Between 169 and 227 of them are inhabited today.

Page 56:
Since 1873, the island's ruins have been excavated and the island itself is cited as an archaeological site.

Page 58:
There is a debate about whether the statue represents Poseidon or Zeus.